OUTER BANKS EDGE

A Photographic Portfolio

Steve Alterman

Sea Glass Publishing, L.L.C.

Outer Banks Edge
A Photographic Portfolio
Steve Alterman

Published in 2013 by Sea Glass Publishing, L.L.C.

Third printing - 2013

ISBN 978-0-9895800-0-7

Design by Sara Birkemeier and George Scott | 8 DOT Graphics
WWW.8DOTGRAPHICS.COM

Printed in China

Cover Photo: Breakers at Pea Island National Wildlife Refuge, taken from an ultralight

CONTENTS

Kitty Hawk Pier at Sunrise
The Day following Hurricane Fran, 1996

FOR LYNNE, LORI AND MARC.

INTRODUCTION

It all began in the spring of 1970. We were young, did not have much money, and we were looking for an inexpensive family vacation. Our neighbors suggested a place wholly unfamiliar to us – the Outer Banks of North Carolina. This simple beginning has grown to a fascination with, and love of, this unique ribbon of sand that stretches from the Virginia border south-southeastward to Cape Hatteras and then abruptly southwesterly across Hatteras Inlet to Ocracoke Island. Exploring these islands and meeting their inhabitants has become a thirty-year obsession.

We soon discovered that the Outer Banks is much more than a summer beach community. Indeed, much of our nation's history is rooted here. The first English colony in the New World was established on Roanoke Island, which became the birthplace of Virginia Dare, the first English child born in America. The Roanoke Island settlers subsequently mysteriously disappeared and forever became "The Lost Colony." Cape Hatteras Lighthouse (built in 1803 and reconstructed in 1870) may be the tallest lighthouse on the East Coast, yet shipwrecks dot the offshore waters. The Civil War ironclad *Monitor,* which sank in 1862, lies below the murky waters off Cape Hatteras, and is the first National Underwater Marine Sanctuary. And the Wright brothers made their historic first flight of a heavier-than-air vehicle from the sand-swept dunes of Kill Devil Hills.

Much has changed since the early 1970s. Development has literally exploded and traffic on Thanksgiving weekend rivals that of the fourth of July. Older buildings have given way to shopping centers and upscale housing developments. This "progress" has altered the Outer Banks considerably, but the basic character remains. Like the colors and patterns of a kaleidoscope, the Outer Banks assaults the senses. The smell of salt air, the pounding of the surf, the colors of the sky, and the presence of the local people, plants and animals all combine to give these barrier islands their ever-changing moods.

The images in this portfolio were taken over the past thirty years. Some photographs depict things no longer in existence – they have either become victims of modern development or have been restored to their original condition. Nevertheless, these images are included in an attempt to convey a feeling of this beautiful part of the United States Eastern Seaboard. Come along and join me on a leisurely trip from Corolla to Ocracoke – stopping along the way wherever, and whenever, there are pictures to be taken.

Self-Portrait, Jockey's Ridge State Park
Nags Head

Currituck Beach Lighthouse
Corolla

Interior, Currituck Beach Lighthouse

Currituck Beach Lighthouse
reflected in Keepers' House Windows

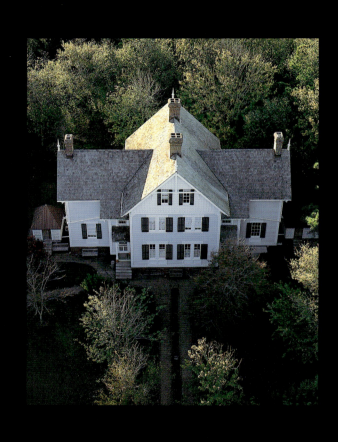

Listed on the National Register of Historic Places, the Lighthouse Keepers' House was constructed of pre-cut materials shipped by barge to Corolla in 1876.

Keepers' House from the top of
Currituck Beach Lighthouse

Footbridge at The Whalehead Club
Corolla

Currituck Beach Lighthouse
through The Whalehead Club Bridge

The Whalehead Club

is part of the

Currituck Heritage

Park in Corolla.

Wild Horses and Egret
behind The Whalehead Club

Fourth of July Fireworks
at The Whalehead Club

Winter Sunset
Corolla

Shipwreck Fragment
Sanderling

Afternoon Sea Oats
Duck

Duck Sunrise

Lost Horizon
Duck

Duck was
incorporated
as a town
in 2002.

Front Yard Tombstones
Downtown Duck

Soundside Sunset
Duck

Ebb Tide
Kitty Hawk

Cottage Detail
Kitty Hawk

Beach Driftwood and Cottages in the Fog
Kitty Hawk

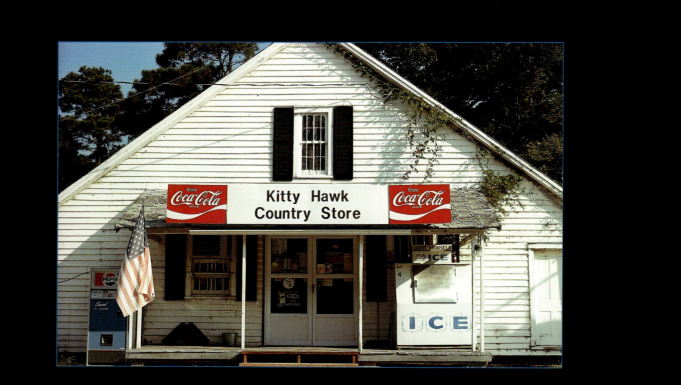

As recently as the 1970s,

many Outer Banks residents

traveled to Elizabeth City to

shop for groceries.

Former Kitty Hawk Country Store

Wright Brothers National Memorial
and Monument Door Detail
Kill Devil Hills

First Flight Takeoff and Landing Sites
Wright Brothers National Memorial

Springtime
Nags Head Woods Ecological Preserve

Autumn Pond and Box Turtle
Nags Head Woods Ecological Preserve

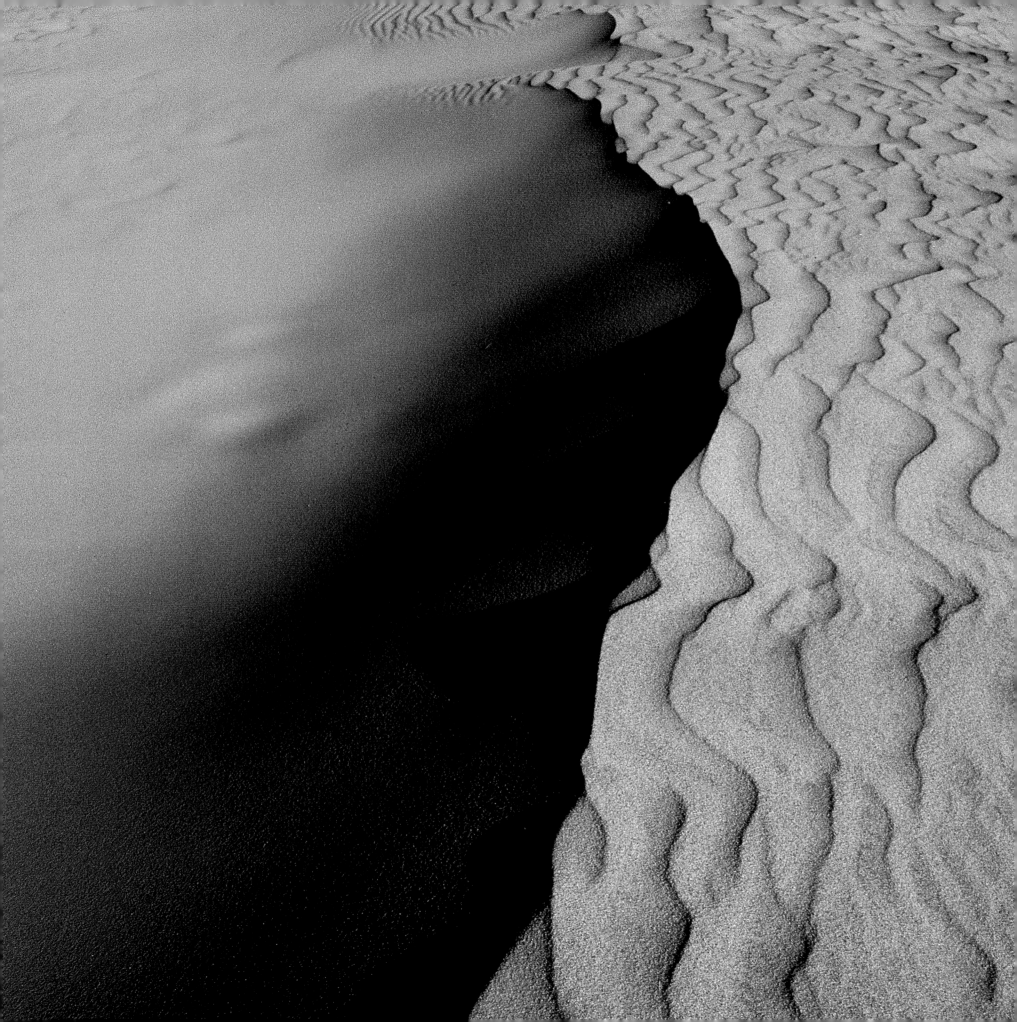

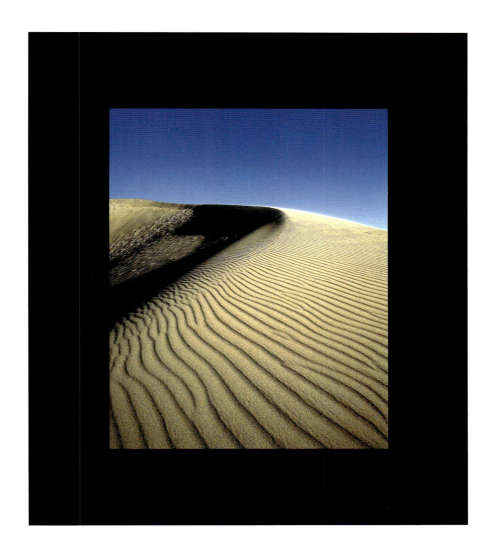

Dune Patterns, Jockey's Ridge State Park
Nags Head

Chasing the Wind, Jockey's Ridge State Park

More than one million

people per year

visit Jockey's Ridge,

the East Coast's

tallest sand dune.

Hang Gliding, Jockey's Ridge State Park

Shifting Sands, Miniature Golf Course Castle
Jockey's Ridge State Park

Sand Fence Pattern and Ghost Crab
Nags Head

Summer Storms
Nags Head

On the Beach
Nags Head

Bodyboarding
Nags Head

Washington Baum Bridge
to Roanoke Island

Wanchese Waterfront

Fish Scales and the *Captain Pete*
Wanchese Harbor

Boat Graveyard
Wanchese

Old Plymouth
Wanchese Garage

Founded by George Washington Creef,

Ye Olde Pioneer Theatre is the oldest

theater in this country continuously

operated by the same family.

Building Mural, Ye Olde Pioneer Theatre
Manteo

The White Doe Inn
Manteo

George Washington Creef Boat Shop
Manteo

October Morning
South Nags Head

Foggy Marsh and a Flurry of Gulls
South Nags Head

Bodie Island Marsh, Late Fall
South Nags Head

Bodie Island Lighthouse

Window Detail and
Hurricane Dennis Floodwaters, 1999
Bodie Island Lighthouse

Gull in Winter Surf
Hatteras Island

Pea Island Breakers and Dune Detail
Pea Island National Wildlife Refuge
Hatteras Island

Chicamacomico Life Saving Station
Rodanthe

Cape Hatteras Lighthouse, Early Morning
Buxton

Towering one hundred

and eighty feet over the sand,

Cape Hatteras Lighthouse

is the tallest in the nation.

Cape Hatteras Lighthouse, Sunrise

Aboard the Hatteras–Ocracoke Ferry
Hatteras Inlet and Pamlico Sound

Silver Lake
Ocracoke

Ocracoke Inlet Lighthouse
Morning Glories on an Ocracoke Barn

Ocracoke Wave

AFTERWORD

Since *Outer Banks Edge* is a book of photography, we consciously decided not to interrupt the flow of the images with unnecessary text. Instead, only captions identify each photo. At the same time, some of the photos and the reasons for their inclusion probably need some explanation. Following are some of the stories behind the pictures.

COROLLA. Today Corolla is a major tourist destination. As recently as 1983, access to the northern Outer Banks was limited, with a gatehouse at the line separating Dare and Currituck counties, and permission needed to travel the dirt road north of Sanderling. The paved road now ends at the Villages at Ocean Hill, just north of the Currituck Beach Lighthouse, although several communities on up to the Virginia border are accessible by driving a four-wheel-drive vehicle on the beach.

In the 1920s, industrialist Edward Collings Knight Jr. built the hunt club mansion Corolla Island — now known as The Whalehead Club — for his wife, Marie Louise (page 23). According to local lore, Mrs. Knight was an avid shooter who had been denied membership to other Currituck County hunt clubs simply because she was a woman. After years of neglect, The Whalehead Club has now been restored to its former glory.

Another Corolla focal point is the Currituck Beach Lighthouse. It is the only unpainted lighthouse on the Outer Banks, with an exterior of solid red brick. While the exterior is beautiful in itself, no one should miss the opportunity to visit the heart of the structure, as shown on pages 12 and 13. Lighthouse interiors are composed of a sensuous swirl of iron and brick, and the view from the top is often breathtaking.

SHIPWRECKS. The Outer Banks is known as "The Graveyard of the Atlantic," and for good reason. More than six hundred shipwrecks lie off the coast, most near the treacherous waters of Diamond Shoals off of Cape Hatteras. This volume has no pictures of shipwrecks, but the image on page 31 is pretty close. This detailed photo shows a section of a *very* old ship (with planks fastened by wooden pegs instead of nails) that washed up in the Sanderling area in the early 1990s. I discovered it on a Sunday morning and it was gone with the tide by Monday.

DUCK. Strange name for a town…it owes its moniker to the numbers of waterfowl that descended in swarms in the years before development. With the Atlantic Ocean on one side and Currituck Sound on the other, Duck is prime sunrise and sunset territory (see pages 34, 35, 40 and 41). If you sleep too late or eat dinner at the "wrong" time, you just might miss a world-class light show.

KITTY HAWK. No, this was *not* the town from which the Wright brothers made their historic flight. It was, however, the location of the post office from which the brothers sent a telegram announcing their success.

The photo of the Kitty Hawk Country Store on page 48 could not have been taken today. A victim of "progress," the structure no longer stands in its former location on Kitty Hawk Road west of Route 158. If you do drive down Kitty Hawk Road today, you will discover a number of creeks and inlets that give residents access to the sound. The image of the pink wildflowers on page 51 was taken in this area.

KILL DEVIL HILLS. Kill Devil Hills was the area from which Orville and Wilbur Wright lifted off in their first powered flight of a heavier-than-air vehicle on December 17, 1903. The Wrights chose this area specifically for its sandy terrain and the constant winds of an Outer Banks winter. Today, this historic site is marked by the Wright Brothers National Memorial, pictured on page 52.

NAGS HEAD. Nags Head's beaches are prime family vacation destinations from early spring to late autumn, with a nearly endless variety of activities (pages 76 and 79). A somewhat hidden treasure occupies the sound side: the Nags Head Woods Ecological Preserve, which is managed by The Nature Conservancy. This maritime forest contains miles of hiking trails through evergreen and deciduous trees, with ponds sprinkled liberally throughout (pages 56 through 63).

Nags Head is also home to Jockey's Ridge State Park, the tallest sand dune on the East Coast. These migrating sands are home to an active hang-gliding community (pages 67 and 68) and presently bury a once-active miniature golf course. The castle pictured on page 71 is the last remaining visible relic of this family activity.

JANUARY 1, 2000. While most of the East Coast was asleep after celebrating New Years Eve, I was out trying to capture the Outer Banks on the first day of the year 2000. The images of the marsh in the early morning fog on page 99 and the *Captain Pete* at rest in Wanchese Harbor on page 84 were taken that morning.

WANCHESE. Wanchese is a small fishing community on Roanoke Island's south side. The harbor photos speak for themselves, but how about the old Plymouth on page 88? This car was rotting in the same garage for as long as I can remember. At the point that the image included in Outer Banks Edge was taken, it was picturesque. Now it is gone.

MANTEO. The county seat of Dare County, Manteo is significantly different from the beach and fishing communities that dot the Outer Banks. It has a courthouse and a business district, as well as residential areas and tourist facilities. The images on pages 91 through 95 are my attempt to capture this area's unique flavor.

HATTERAS ISLAND. Across the Bonner Bridge, which spans Oregon Inlet, is Hatteras Island, home to the famous Cape Hatteras Lighthouse and miles of National Seashore. Driving south through Hatteras Island, you'll spot the restored Chicamacomico Lifesaving Station (pages 110 and 111), which stands as a memorial to the maritime heroes who rescued those stranded by the sea.

North Carolina's state symbol is the Cape Hatteras Lighthouse. All of the images in this volume were taken in its former location, which was virtually on the beach in Buxton (pages 112, 113 and 115). The lighthouse has since been moved 1,600 feet inland to protect it from the Atlantic's pounding waves. It's a lot safer now – but not nearly as photogenic!

OCRACOKE. Our photographic journey ends on Ocracoke Island, a short ferry ride from Hatteras Village. Twelve miles of unspoiled beaches lead to Ocracoke Village, with its quaint harbor and short white lighthouse. The barn on page 121 used to stand next to the Ocracoke Inlet Lighthouse and is another victim of old age.

S.A.

Sand Fence
South Nags Head

ACKNOWLEDGMENTS

Left to my own devices, this book would never have been produced or published. This third printing is the product of the work of a talented group of individuals who encouraged me to keep *Outer Banks Edge* on the region's bookshelves.

Primary contributors have been Sara Birkemeier and George Scott of 8 Dot Graphics who are the brains behind the book's design and Nancy and Richard LaMotte of Sea Glass Publishing who have led me through the reprinting process. In addition, it would be difficult to overstate the contribution of all the Outer Banks booksellers who have been instrumental in selling our two previous printings. Special thanks go to Allen Lehew and Jamie Layton of Duck's Cottage who not only sell the book, but also provide my morning coffee, and to Bill Rickman of Island Bookstore who is always asking for more copies!

Thanks to all of you!
Steve Alterman